# Learn HTML, CSS, and JavaScript With This One Book

Please note; that this book is just the CSS chapter of the full book; the **Basics of Front-End Web Development (HTML, CSS, and JavasScript)**. To learn all three coding languages, check out the full book.

https://www.amazon.com/Basics-Front-End-Development-HTML-JavaScript-ebook/dp/B0DJ147B15

# Learn SEO Too

Learning front-end web development is only half the battle to producing an amazing web experience. Also, you need to learn **SEO (search engine optimization)**.

Learning SEO ensures that visitors can actually find your website and apps on the internet. Below I included links to several SEO books I've written. They are excellent reads.

**The ABCs of SEO: Search Engine Optimization 101**

https://www.amazon.com/ABCs-Search-Engine-Optimization-Page-ebook/dp/B0C2JSLW7M

**The Technical SEO Handbook**

https://www.amazon.com/Technical-SEO-Handbook-Learn-Issues-ebook/dp/B0CMBJR9QV

**The SEO and Web Developer Collaboration Guide**

https://www.amazon.com/SEO-Web-Developer-Collaboration-Guide-ebook/dp/B0DHLBM48C

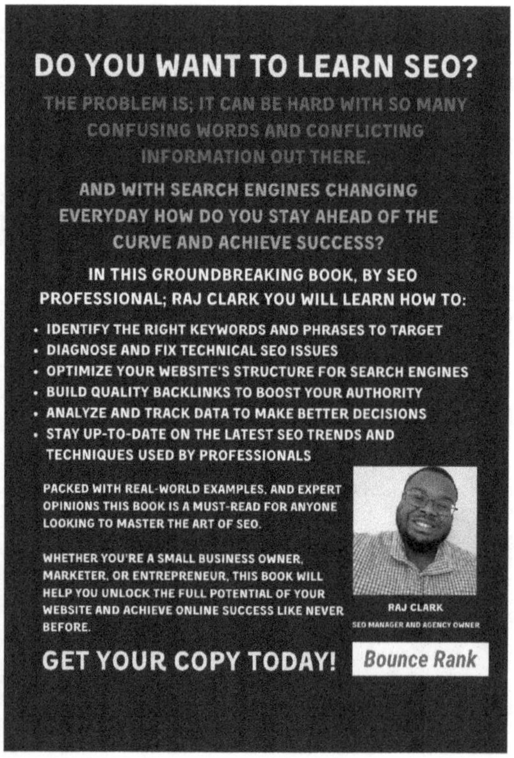

# The Basics of CSS (Cascading Style Sheets) Coding For Beginners

By: Roggie Clark

# Copyright

Title: The Basics of CSS (Cascading Style Sheets) Coding For Beginners
Author: Roggie Clark



Cover Design: Roggie Clark
Editing: Renee' Clark

Printed in the United States of America

# Disclaimer

The views and opinions expressed in this book are those of the author and do not necessarily reflect the official policy or position of any individual, company, or organization cited or referenced in the text.

The author is not affiliated with any of the individuals, companies, or organizations mentioned in the text, nor does the author receive any form of compensation for citing or referencing them. Some sample scenarios in this text are fictitious. Any similarity to actual persons, living or dead, is coincidental.

The professional information (strategies, tips, and concepts) in this text is distributed on an "as is" basis, without warranty. While every precaution has been taken in the preparation of the text to ensure all information is accurate, neither the author nor the publisher shall have any liability to any person or entity with respect to any loss or damage caused or alleged to be caused directly or indirectly by the instructions contained in this text or by the computer software and hardware products described in it.

Neither the author nor the publisher guarantees any specific results or outcomes, and the information provided in this text should not be construed as professional advice. Readers should always consult with a qualified professional before making any significant changes to their website or business.

By reading this text, you agree that the author nor the publisher is responsible for any direct, indirect, incidental, or consequential damages that may arise from the use of the information provided. You assume full responsibility for any actions taken based on the information presented in this text.

# Table of Contents

# Chapter 1: Introduction

Rev up you're engines! You are about to take a drive down the exciting road of website development! Think of your website's HTML as a basic frame of a car, boring, and simple, but with CSS (Cascading Style Sheets) you can take this basic frame and make it into a sleek, bright car guaranteed to make heads turn!

CSS isn't just about making websites look nice; no it's so much more - it's what makes them come alive! By controlling their design and layout, it allows developers the opportunity to move beyond simple content and create a true user experience that is sure to please.

CSS has so many amazing features like flexboxes, grids, color profiles, and fonts, that help structure and design an amazing web experience. Whether you're creating a blog, showcasing your portfolio, or refining the look of the next big app, CSS is where your creativity can really take off.

**Here's what you'll be able to do once you learn just the basics of CSS:**

- Build stunning, professional-looking websites that reflect your exact vision.

- Fine-tune every detail, from fonts and colors to layouts and animations, giving your site a unique identity.

- Make sure your designs look amazing across all devices, from smartphones to desktops.

- Combine CSS with HTML and JavaScript to create smooth, dynamic web experiences.

The best part about CSS is, that it is a beginner-friendly coding language that can be picked up in as little as 2 weeks, even if you're new to coding. You don't need to be a design expert to create something beautiful. With a few basic principles and some practice, you'll be amazed by what you can build.

By the end of this book, not only will you know how to create websites, but you'll also have the skills to make them stand out in the vast online world. Okay, let's get into Chapter 2 which is the basics of CSS concepts and syntax.

# Chapter 2: Cascading Style Sheets (CSS) Concepts

Co-created by Norwegian web developer Håkon Wium Lie and Dutch computer scientist Bert Bos, **Cascading Style Sheets (CSS)** was released in 1996 as a new programming language used to "style" or change the appearance of HTML elements, to make them more visually appealing to the reader (Wikipedia, n.d.).

With CSS, you can control many aspects of the look and feel of an HTML webpage including text size, text color, font type, background color, borders, margins, etc.

The instructions that the browsers use to accurately display the style of these elements are stored in documents called "Stylesheets". The name "Cascading" comes from the ability of one style sheet to inherit or overwrite the styles of another or *Cascade* (Hoffman, 2017).

CSS is considered to be a "declarative" programming language, meaning that it gives the web browser *suggestions* on how to display the elements on the webpage; but does not assert *exactly* how to display them. (Britannica, n.d.). This unique functionality of CSS makes it one of the most widely used tools in web design and development today.

## CSS Syntax

Just like HTML, to write CSS properly, there are a few things you should consider, following these syntax rules will ensure that your code is correct, easy to read, and can be used multiple times. Here are the syntax rules:

### 1. CSS Syntax Structure:

CSS consists of two main components: **selectors** and **declarations**.

- A **selector** identifies the HTML element you want to style.
- A **declaration** specifies the style to be applied.

Declarations are written inside **curly braces** `{ }` and consist of a **property** and a **value**, separated by a colon (`:`). Each declaration ends with a semicolon (`;`).

**Basic Structure of CSS:**

```
selector {
  property: value;
}
```

**Example:**

```
h1 {
  color: blue;
  font-size: 24px;
}
```

**In this example:**

- `h1` is the selector (it targets all `<h1>` elements).
- `color: blue;` is a declaration that changes the text color to blue.
- `font-size: 24px;` sets the font size to 24 pixels.

---

### 2. Selectors and Specificity:

- Different types of **Selectors** can also be used to determine which HTML elements get styled. Common types include:
  - **Type selectors** (e.g., `p`) target elements by name.
  - **Class selectors** (e.g., `.classname`) target elements with a specific class. The `.` is used to indicate that a class selector is being used.
  - **ID selectors** (e.g., `#idname`) target elements with a unique ID. The `#` is used to indicate that an ID selector is being used.
- **Specificity** determines which style is applied if multiple rules conflict:
  - IDs have higher specificity than classes, which have higher specificity than type selectors.
  - Inline styles `(style="...")` have the highest specificity. (we will explore inline styles in greater detail in the *How CSS is Added to HTML Section.*

---

### 3. Cascading and Inheritance:

- As I said earlier, CSS stands for **Cascading Style Sheets** because the styles "cascade" down. Because of this, if multiple rules apply to an element, the rule with the highest specificity or the rule declared last takes precedence. So if the rule is an ID it will take precedence over a Class. While a Class would take precedence over a Type.
- Some properties are **inherited** `(e.g., font-family)`, meaning they are passed down from parent elements to child elements. Others, like `margin` or `border`, are not

inherited. We will explore these properties in greater detail in the *Common CSS Properties* section

---

**4. Box Model:**

- Every HTML element can be thought of as a **box**. Understanding the **box model** is crucial for layout. The box consists of **content**, **padding**, **border**, and **margin,** below I included an image of what the box model looks like, this will help you with using it**:**

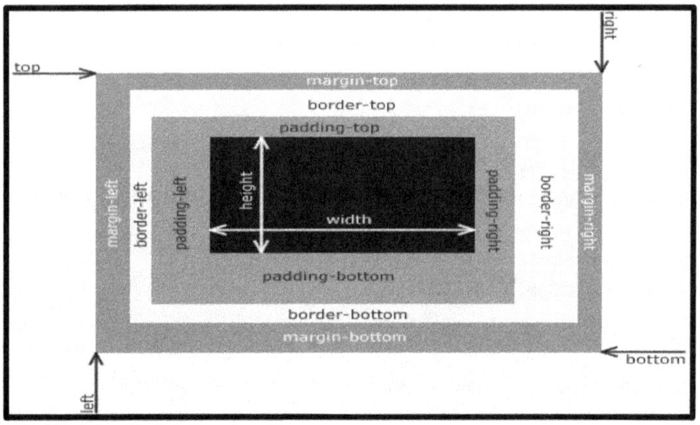


**Cite:https://en.wikipedia.org/wiki/CSS_box_model**

**Example:**

```
article {

  margin: 10px;

  padding: 20px;

  border: 1px solid black;

}
```

---

**5. Units and Measurements:**

- CSS uses a variety of units for lengths and sizes:
  - **Pixels** (`px`) are fixed units. For example, `10px`
  - **Percentages** (`%`) are relative to a parent container's size. E.g `10%`

- **Ems** (`em`) and **rem** are relative units based on font size (useful for responsive design). E.g `10em` or `1rem`

- For responsive designs, relative units like `%`, `em`, and `rem` are preferred over fixed `px`.

---

### 6. Shorthand Properties:

- CSS has many **shorthand properties** that allow you to set multiple values at once, reducing the amount of code you write.

**Example:**

```
/* Longhand */

margin-top: 10px;

margin-right: 20px;

margin-bottom: 10px;

margin-left: 20px;


/* Shorthand */

margin: 10px 20px;
```

---

### 7. Pseudo Classes:

A **CSS pseudo-class** is a keyword added to selectors that specifies a special state of an element. Pseudo-classes are used to style elements based on dynamic factors like user interaction or position within the document, even though they might not be distinguishable through standard attributes.

**For example, a pseudo-class can apply styles when:**

- The user hovers over a link (`:hover`)
- A form input is focused (`:focus`)
- A link has been visited (`:visited`)

- The first child of an element is selected (`:first-child`)

Here's an example of using the `:hover` pseudo-class to change the color of a link when a user hovers over it:

```
a:hover {

  color: red;

}
```

In this case, when the user moves the mouse over a link, its color will change to red. Pseudo-classes are very useful for creating interactive designs and improving the user experience without requiring JavaScript.

---

**8. Commenting:**

- Comments in CSS are written with `/* */` and can help make your code more readable and easier to maintain.

**Example:**

```
/* This styles the heading */

h1 {

  color: blue; }
```

# Chapter 3: Common CSS Properties

Now that we explored CSS syntax in detail let's now go over other examples of common CSS properties you may encounter:

**1. Color and Background:**

- `color:` Sets the text color. **Example:** `{color: #333;}`
- `background-color:` Specifies the background color of an element. **Example:** `{background-color: #f5f5f5;}`
- `background-image:` Adds an image as the background of an element. Be sure to add url of the image you wish to add. **E.g;** `background-image: url('image.jpg');`

---

**2. Typography:**

- `font-family:` Specifies the font type.
  **Example:** `{font-family: 'Arial', sans-serif;}`
- `font-size:` Defines the size of the text.
  **Example:** `{font-size: 16px;}`
- `font-weight:` Controls the boldness of the text.
  **Example:** `{font-weight: bold;}`
- `text-align:` Aligns text horizontally (left, center, right). **Example:** `{text-align: center;}`
- `line-height:` Controls the space between lines of text. **Example:** `{line-height: 1.5;}`

---

**3. Spacing:**

- `margin:` Defines the space outside the element.

**Example:** `{margin: 20px;}`

- `padding:` Defines the space inside the element, between the content and the border.
  **Example:** `{padding: 15px;}`

---

**4. Box Model:**

- `width:` **and** `height:` Set the width and height of an element.
  **Example:**
  ```
  {width: 300px;
  height: 200px;
  }
  ```

- `border:` Adds a border around an element.
  **Example:** `{border: 1px solid #000;}`

- `border-radius:` sets the roundness of corners on the border
  **Example:** `{border-radius: 50px 20px;}`

- `box-shadow:` Adds shadow around an element.
  **Example:** `{border: 1px solid #000;}`

---

**5. Positioning:**

- `position:` Specifies the positioning method (static, relative, absolute, fixed).
  **Example:** `{position: relative;}`

- `top, right, bottom, left:` Offsets an element from its position.
  **Example:** `{top: 10px; left: 20px;}`

---

**6. Display and Layout:**

- `display:` Defines how an element is displayed (block, inline, inline-block, flex).
  **Example:**
  ```
  {display: block;
  display: flex;}
  ```

- `flex:` Enables flexbox layout properties for easier element alignment.
  **Example:** `{display: flex; justify-content: space-between;}`

- `overflow:` Controls how overflowed content is handled (visible, hidden, scroll).
  **Example:** `{overflow: hidden;}`

---

**7. Visibility:**

- `visibility:` Controls the visibility of an element (visible, hidden).
  **Example:** `{visibility: hidden;}`

- `opacity:` Sets the opacity (transparency) of an element.
  css
  **Example:** `{opacity: 0.5;}`

---

**8. Hover Effects:**

- `:hover:` Adds styles to an element when the mouse hovers over it.
  **Example:** `a:hover { color: red;}`

# Chapter 4: Mobile Responsive Design

Producing websites that work seamlessly across mobile devices is now a requirement for a skilled developer in this age. The reason being, search engines only want to send users to websites that are "Mobile responsive".

This matters greatly for SEO, and again to be a great web developer you should definitely learn SEO. So reading this section will help you do it. Let's get into it;

### 1. Fluid Layouts:

- **Use Relative Units**: Instead of fixed units like `px` , use flexible units like percentages `(%)`, `em` , `rem` , or viewport-based units (`vw`, `vh`) for width, margin, padding, etc. This helps elements adapt to different screen sizes.

**Example:**

```
.container {

    width: 80%; /* Adapts to the size of the viewport */

}
```

---

### 2. Media Queries:

- **Adjust Layout Based on Screen Size**: Use media queries to apply different styles for various screen widths. This allows you to design for specific device sizes (mobile, tablet, desktop).

**Example:**

```
@media only screen and (max-width: 768px) {

    .container {

        width: 100%;

        padding: 10px;

    }}
```

### 3. Mobile-First Approach:

- **Design for Small Screens First**: Start by designing for mobile devices, then use media queries to scale up for larger screens. This ensures that the essential content is optimized for smaller, more restrictive devices.

**Example:**

```
/* Default (mobile-first) */

body { font-size: 16px; }


/* For tablets and small desktops */

@media (min-width: 768px) and (max-width: 1024px)

{ body { font-size: 18px; }


/* For large desktops and up */

@media (min-width: 1025px)

{ body { font-size: 20px; } }
```

### 4. Flexible Grid Systems:

- **CSS Grid or Flexbox**: Use these layout systems to create flexible and adaptive grid structures that rearrange themselves based on screen size.

  Below I include an image that I cited showing the difference between a Flexbox and CSS Grid. As you can see the Flexbox is more "one-dimensional" this is for more archaic, static web pages. But with a grid, you can create dynamic layouts that adjust to different screen sizes, this is going to be more important for web app designing.

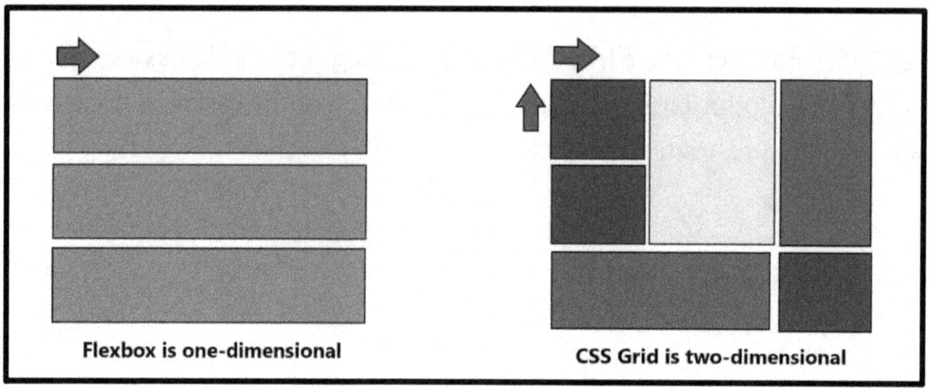


**Cited:**https://www.linkedin.com/pulse/revolutionizing-web-layouts-impact-flexbox-css-grid-razal-kabeer-qr0kf/

**Flexbox Example:**

```
.container {

    display: flex;

    flex-wrap: wrap;

}

.item {

    flex: 1 1 100%;

}

@media (min-width: 600px) {

    .item {

        flex: 1 1 50%;

    }}
```

**CSS Grid Example:**

```
.grid {
    display: grid;
    grid-template-columns: 1fr;
}
@media (min-width: 768px) {
    .grid {
        grid-template-columns: 1fr 1fr;
    }
}
```

---

**5. Viewport Meta Tag:**

- **Set the Viewport for Mobile Devices**: Use the viewport meta tag in the HTML to ensure the browser adjusts the layout properly for mobile screens. If you recall from the *HTML Chapter* this tag is pivotal to having an optimal search engine performance as well, so don't forget it.

**Example:**

```
<meta name="viewport" content="width=device-width, initial-
scale=1.0">
```

---

**6. Responsive Images:**

- **Use `max-width` for Images**: Ensure images resize proportionally by setting a `max-width` of 100% so they don't overflow their container.

**Example:**

```
img {

    max-width: 100%;

    height: auto;

}
```

---

### 7. Hide/Show Content:

- **Display or Hide Elements**: Sometimes, you may need to hide certain elements on smaller screens or show alternative content. You can use media queries to control visibility.

**Example:**

```
.desktop-only {

    display: none;

}

@media (min-width: 1024px) {

    .desktop-only {

        display: block;

    }

}
```

---

### 8. Test on Different Devices:

- **Cross-Device Testing**: Always test your site on different devices or use responsive design tools in browsers to ensure your styles work well across different screen sizes.

---

**9. Touch-Friendly Elements:**

- **Larger Clickable Areas**: Ensure that buttons, links, and interactive elements are large enough and spaced adequately for touch screens. Search engines like Google recommend a minimum touch target size of **48x48 pixels**.

---

**10. CSS Frameworks (Optional):**

- **Use CSS Frameworks**: "CSS frameworks" come with built-in responsive design utilities, grid systems, and pre-designed components that can help accelerate development. However, it's beneficial to understand the underlying principles before relying heavily on frameworks.

## Final Thoughts

Understanding these properties will help you as a beginner create well-structured and visually appealing websites, while also providing a solid foundation to build more advanced designs. In the next section, we are going to explore the different ways in which CSS can be added to an HTML document.

# Chapter 5: How CSS is Added to HTML

CSS can be added to an HTML document generally in three ways: *inline, external,* or *internal*. Each way has pros and cons.

For the explanation of the pros and cons of each, I will be citing web author's; Nikita Hlopov article; *How to include CSS to a page (with Pros and Cons)*.

### Inline CSS

For CSS to be added inline, the *style attribute* `style=""` or a special modifier that allows the CSS file to be referenced is added to the HTML tag or element.
Here's an example from W3school (n.d.):

```
<h1 style="color:blue;">insert text here</h1>
```

As you can see the code snippet includes the HTML element that is to be styled, this is also known as the *selector*. In this case, we are styling the <h1> element. Then an equal sign `=` and quotation marks "" are added to show that you are including a *declaration* that tells the computer to use the style defined in quotation marks.

Next, a *property* is added, which is the name of the style you want to use.

In the code example above, the property is `color` (change the font color).

The property is then followed by a colon `:`, then the *value* or what you want to change the element to.

For color, I wrote `blue`. Lastly, you end the declaration statement with a semicolon `;`

Also as you can see the style modifier is only added to the opening tag `<h1>`, this modifier should never be added to the closing tag `</h1>`

#### Pros and Cons

Here are some pros and cons of inline CSS implementation according to (Hlopov, 2021):

**Pros:**

- Useful for overriding default styling

- Has a higher specificity than any CSS selector (recall this information from the *CSS syntax section*; inline styles are more specific than **ID**, which is more specific than **Class**, which is more specific than **Type**. Also note this can be a Con because it can override more general styling and external stylesheets.

**Cons:**
- Not an easy way to apply styling for the whole page, especially if it's large
- Has a higher specificity than any CSS selector which can override external stylesheets
- Hard to manage and maintain.

---

## External CSS

CSS can also be applied through an *external* file with the **.CSS** extension and then load it within a web page with an `<link>` HTML tag, and a `rel` and `href` attribute added to the link tag.

**Here's an example:**

```
<head>
  <link rel="stylesheet" href="styles.css">
</head>
```

As you can see the code; `<link rel="stylesheet" href="styles.css">` was nested in `<head>` tag.

The `<link>` tag indicates that a file is being called or located from another document. The `rel` attribute is used to indicate what type of file is to be requested, in this case a `stylesheet`. Then the `href` attribute indicates the name of the stylesheet file in this case, `styles.css` (W3school, n.d.).

You may be wondering, what does the `styles.css` file look like?

Here's a `styles.css` code snippet:

```
h1 {
  color: red;
```

```
}
```

In the code snippet, you can also see the HTML element that is to be styled. Again, in this case, the selector is added, `<h1>` element, followed by curly brackets `{ }` to indicate the start of the declaration. The `color` property is again added.

Then the property is again followed by a colon `:` then the "value" or what you want the property to be is added. For color, I added `red` and then ended the declaration statement with a semicolon `;`

Now, here are the pros and cons of using external CSS, according to (Hlopov, 2021):

**Pros and Cons**

**Pros**:

- All styles are stored in one separate file, making it easier to manage and maintain;
- Ability to include multiple different files if needed;
- Comments can be added to be interpretation easier for different developers
- The CSS file can be minified meaning decreased size in bytes. (This matters for SEO)

**Cons**:

- Linking external files creates render-blocking content which affects the rate and speed that Search engines can crawl and index web pages. Additionally, this can lead to a poor user experience because it may take visitors longer to access the website (Again this matters for SEO).
- May contain styles that are not used on a particular page, thus loading unused code. Which again can slow the rate and speed at which the website can be accessed and crawled by search engines.

---

## Internal CSS

Lastly, we have internal CSS. Internal CSS is deployed using the `<style>` element nested in the `<head>` tag, again if you recall the `<head>` tag is generally where non-viewable/ non-interactive web elements are stored.

Next, nested in the `<style>` element is the *selector* or the element name that is to be styled is then included, in this case, it is the H2 tag `<h2>` again followed by curly brackets `{ }` to indicate the start of a declaration and then the property you want to style.

**Here's an example:**

```
<head>
    <style>
        H2 {
            Color: green;
            font-family: times new roman

            font-weight: bold;
            }
    </style>
</head>
```

In the code example, there are two new properties: `font-family` (changes the font type), and `font-weight` (Changes the thinness or thickness of the font).

The declaration is then followed by a colon `:`, then the value or what you want the property to be is added.

For `color`, I wrote `green`, for `font-family,` I wrote `times new roman`, and for `font-weight`, I wrote `bold`, to indicate I want the font to be thick. You end the declaration statement with a semicolon `;`

Now, let's review the pros and cons, again to recall (Hlopov, 2021):

### Pros and Cons

**Pros:**

- Useful for overriding default styling;

- Can be turned on and off with JavaScript;
- Can be used to contain default minimum styling if the main stylesheet is being loaded asynchronously.

**Cons:**

- Not a very convenient way to apply styling for the whole page, especially if it's large;
- Hard to manage and maintain.

---

# Chapter 6: Practice Activities

Now that you've learned the basics of CSS, it's time to test your understanding with some hands-on practice. Practice is essential for mastering web development, and the more you experiment with CSS, the more you'll solidify the concepts you've learned.

In this chapter, we will present a series of exercises that focus on key CSS concepts like styling text, layout techniques, colors, spacing, and positioning. These exercises are designed to help you build real-world web pages with enhanced styling. By completing them, you'll gain confidence in applying your CSS knowledge to actual projects.

### 1. Styling Text with CSS

**Question:** Create a simple webpage and use CSS to style the text in the following ways:

- A heading that says "Styled Text" with a font size of 36px.
- A paragraph with the sentence: "CSS allows us to style text with colors, fonts, and more."
- Make the text color of the heading blue, and set the paragraph font to italic and the color to dark gray.

**Hint:** Use CSS properties like `font-size`, `color`, `font-style`, and `font-family` to style your text.

### 2. Background Colors and Borders

**Question:** Create a webpage where you apply background colors and borders to elements:

- A section with the background color light blue.
- A paragraph inside the section with a 2px solid border in black.
- Add padding of 20px inside the paragraph to create space between the text and the border.

**Hint:** Use `background-color`, `border`, and `padding` properties in your CSS to achieve this.

### 3. Centering Elements

**Question:** Create a webpage that includes the following:

- A heading that says "Centering with CSS."

- Center the heading horizontally on the page using CSS.
- Add a button below the heading that is also centered on the page.

**Hint:** Use `text-align: center;` for the heading and a combination of `display: flex` and `justify-content: center` for centering the button.

### 4. Creating a Navigation Bar

**Question:** Create a simple navigation bar for your webpage:

- The navigation bar should contain links to "Home," "About," and "Contact."
- Style the navigation links so that they are displayed horizontally, with some space between them.
- When hovering over the links, change the background color to light gray.

**Hint:** Use `display: inline-block` or `display: flex` for horizontal alignment and the `:hover` pseudo-class for hover effects.

### 5. Box Model Practice

**Question:** Create a webpage with a content box that demonstrates the CSS box model:

- A box with a width of 300px and a height of 150px.
- Apply a solid border of 4px, padding of 20px, and margin of 30px around the box.
- Set a background color of your choice for the box.

**Hint:** Use `width`, `height`, `border`, `padding`, `margin`, and `background-color` properties.

### 6. Flexbox Layout

**Question:** Create a webpage layout using Flexbox:

- A header at the top of the page with the text "Flexbox Layout."
- A main section with two columns: one for navigation and one for the main content.
- Make sure the navigation and main content are displayed side-by-side and evenly spaced.

**Hint:** Use `display: flex` and properties like `flex-basis`, `flex-grow`, and `justify-content` to structure the layout.

### 7. Adding Shadows and Rounded Corners

**Question:** Create a card element with a shadow and rounded corners:

- The card should have a heading with the text "My Card" and a paragraph with some placeholder text.
- Apply a shadow around the card and round the corners.
- Add some padding inside the card for better spacing.

**Hint:** Use `box-shadow`, `border-radius`, and `padding` properties.

### 8. Responsive Web Design

**Question:** Create a responsive layout that adjusts on smaller screens:

- A container with two sections side-by-side when viewed on a desktop.
- On a mobile device (screen width less than 600px), the two sections should stack vertically.

**Hint:** Use `@media` queries and Flexbox or Grid layout to create a responsive design.

### 9. CSS Grid Layout

**Question:** Create a webpage using CSS Grid to create a layout with three sections:

- A header at the top, a content area with two columns, and a footer at the bottom.
- Use CSS Grid to position these elements and ensure they are aligned properly.

**Hint:** Use `display: grid` and properties like `grid-template-columns`, `grid-template-rows`, and `grid-gap` to create the layout.

### 10. Animating Elements

**Question:** Create a simple webpage with an animation effect:

- A button that says "Click Me."
- When hovered over, the button should change color smoothly over half a second.

**Hint:** Use the `transition` property for smooth animation, and the `:hover` pseudo-class to trigger the color change.

## Conclusion

These 10 practice activities are designed to cover a range of essential CSS skills, from text styling and layout techniques to responsive design and animations. By working through these exercises, you will reinforce what you have learned and start applying CSS to real-world scenarios.

As you complete each task, review the output in your browser to ensure that the CSS behaves as expected. Remember: mastering CSS takes practice. The more you work through exercises like these, the more comfortable you'll become with styling and designing webpages, setting the foundation for more advanced topics like animations and CSS frameworks.

# Chapter 7: Last Thoughts

As we come to the conclusion of this journey, it's important to step back and reflect on what you've learned about the essential components of web development—CSS.

**CSS (Cascading Style Sheets)** is the design language of the web. While HTML provides the structure, CSS is what gives a website its visual presentation, transforming plain content into a visually engaging experience. Everything from colors, fonts, spacing, and layout is controlled by CSS, allowing you to craft a unique look and feel for each webpage.

By learning CSS, you've acquired the skills to style and enhance web content in ways that improve both aesthetics and usability. You've explored different CSS properties, from text formatting and backgrounds to layout techniques like Flexbox and Grid. You've learned how to make websites responsive, adapting designs for various screen sizes and devices. These are the essential tools that allow you to style and format any website.

Learning CSS is like learning design principles—it gives you the power to shape how users interact with a site visually. But like any skill, mastery comes with continuous practice and exploration. There's always something new to learn—whether it's refining your understanding of CSS animations, exploring newer layout techniques, or experimenting with different design systems.

The best way to improve your CSS skills is by applying them to real-world projects. Start with smaller projects like personal portfolios or simple landing pages, where you can experiment with different design choices. Over time, you can tackle more complex challenges like multi-page websites or custom layouts, using advanced techniques such as CSS Grid or custom properties (CSS variables).

Each project will help you grow as a designer, whether it's discovering new ways to organize your styles or finding more efficient methods to create responsive designs. The more you build, the more deeply you'll understand how CSS shapes the user experience.

Remember, web development isn't just about coding—it's also about creativity, problem-solving, and an ongoing commitment to learning. Keep experimenting, keep refining your styles, and most importantly, enjoy the creative process.

Thank you for joining me on this journey. The web is a vast space with endless opportunities for creativity and innovation. Now, it’s your turn to take what you've learned and style something incredible!

## About the Author

Roggie (Raj) Clark, is a 9 year SEO professional and owner of the SEO agency; *Bounce Rank.* Prior to joining the SEO industry, Raj was a web developer and school teacher. It was through creating his own websites, and wanting a career change from teaching, that Raj stumbled across the world of SEO.

Since joining the field nearly a decade ago, Raj has worked on a wide range of campaigns, from eCommerce, to B2B, to Healthcare, for enterprise companies and marketing agencies in the United States.

He is regarded as an expert, and guru by his colleagues, and the SEO industry. Raj currently lives in Maryland with his sister and niece.

www.ingramcontent.com/pod-product-compliance
Lightning Source LLC
LaVergne TN
LVHW080001210926
848481LV00012B/3648